The Hope I've Learned

Carson Clayson

BookLeaf Publishing

Presentation by *BookLeaf Publishing*

Web: www.bookleafpub.com

E-mail: info@bookleafpub.com

ISBN: 9789395756341

First edition 2022

DEDICATION

For my Mom and Dad, who gave me the greatest gift parents can give, a happy family and a foundation of faith.

ACKNOWLEDGEMENT

Special thanks to my friend Emma who told me about this challenge. As well as my many friends and leaders from the New Hampshire Manchester Mission who suggested I put my poems into a book.

New

I'll try something
New
Stepping from what I know

Into the fog.

And hear,
O thou perfectionist
Who dwells in my heart
And tugs at the strings,

I am the captain of my soul
And you will not stop me
From failing.

I will fail
Gloriously;
Royally flunk
And fall in the mud,
Only to rise,
Dripping in desire
To try again.

Hear, O my heart,
You are strong,
You can heal and move on.

Neither pain of failure
Nor the halting of indecision
Will stop you from succeeding
For it is from the ashes of defeat
That every phoenix rises.

Why Life is Hard

Trees grow deeper with a breeze,
Muscles grow stronger with work,
And minds grow sharper with study.

Is it any question, then, why life is hard?
Opposition yields opportunity
Resistance yields results
And training yields triumph.

This world, then, was not made
By some cruel being.
No, you aren't simply here
To be beaten senseless
And sent to oblivion.
Though at times you may feel that way.

(K)no(w), there is hope.

When life leaves you lifeless,
When the world leaves you writhing,
On the side of some obscure road,
In a far more obscure country,

You can have hope through a kind stranger,
A good Samaritan of sorts;
Better known as a physician,
A carpenter,
A Savior,
Who will pick you up and carry you to safety;
Who will put you in an inn,
and pay for your safekeeping.
He is a physician, to bind your wounds,
A carpenter to build your soul,
A Savior to set you back on the road,
Stronger than you were before.

The Son of God can take your weakness,
Your wounds and your scars
And replace them with strength, with healing,
and with love.
Through Jesus Christ
Your roots can weather the storms,
Your arms can bare the load,
Your mind can fill with joy.

Jesus has come to me,
In my hour of need.
I trust that life yet
Has tricks up its sleeve
Specifically set for me,
But I trust yet more,
That my Savior and Lord

Has everything I need,
For me to endure.
I know too that He has great glory
For you in store.

Mansions, thrones, and crowns,
If you seek his help
And heed his word.

Please, in faith seek,
And you shall find
Without doubt, knock
and it shall open up to you,
Ask with trust in God
and it shall be given to you.

Hope's Last String

(Inspired by George Watts' painting "Hope")

There she was, alone.
Her name, Hope.
Her status, hopeless,
Nearly.

There she was, blindfolded,
Because sight brought her pain
And dimmed her hearing.

There she was, filled
With desire to bring good
To a world deafened by evil.

There she was, strumming
On the final unbroken string
Of an ancient, holy harp.

There they fell beside her,
Tears, streaming behind the blindfold
As she strummed out one tone.
She wanted so deeply
To play the world a melody
But she gave them everything she had

And wept, when all she had
Was one note over and over.

As the day rolled on,
The tears slowed
And she stroked on.
Intently, she listened
To all that she had.
Sometimes she played slowly,
And listened to see
How long the note last.
One time, she played quickly,
Strumming the air
To the tune of her favorite song.
She could hear it,
The full richness
Of a complete harp's song,
Even though the air was still.
But then came the part
Where she hit that last string.
Without warning,
Without preamble,
And with one painful sound
Hope's last hope broke.

There she was, alone.
Alone and numb.
The joy of her imagined song
Fell utterly flat,

And so for a long while she sat.
Alone and numb.
Hopeless.

Until a drip fell on her head.

She looked to the sky and cried,
"My God, why?
Why did you let every single string break
From the first to the last?
My God, why?
Why did you let the light leave
Every single land?
My God, why?
Why am I yet here in the dark
When you give light to every man?"

She wept and sat for hours,
Thinking she wasn't heard.
But then there came a whisper,
"Open your eyes"
It shook Hope to her core.
She could do nothing for the shock of it.
"Open your eyes and see me,"
Came the voice again.
It was a voice she knew,
Though long had it been
Since it had graced her ears.
It was the voice of God.

"Open your eyes,
For I have heard your prayer."

She lifted her blindfold and saw
Beauty manifest
A God with eyes like fire
Hair of brilliant gold,
The skin of shining bronze,
But most beautiful of all,
His hands held a harp.
"My dearest Hope,"
Spake the Lord,
"I sent you into the world
To be a light unto it.
I gave you that harp
To know you'd play
With all your heart.
Now I ask of you to play
This heavenly harp
And bring the day
To a world locked in dark."

Hope took the golden harp
From the hands of her God
And played with all her heart.
To her it was as though
The day of restoration came
Each note brought life
To her weak and wearied soul.

Each strum gave light
To passersby,
And to they who hid
Out of sight.
They came to Hope
With broken bows
Shattered flutes
And worn violas.
The God of music
And God of Hope
Gave each listener
New instruments
To play with Hope
In her soft tune,
First one,
Then a few,
And with time they grew and grew.
Together they shined
Like the sun and moon.
The world once dark
Was brighter than our noon.

When you feel like Hope,
Hopeless
Keep playing the tune,
Even if all you have
Is the least and last string
On a pitiful harp.
Give all you have,

Till all you have is gone
And then from heaven will come
The God of Hope
And His Holy Son.
Your faith and hope
Will be returned
And you will see
That these trials have meaning
They prepare us to give light
To everything.

The Weight of the World

The pressure came in at all angles
"Be perfect
In every movement,
Be perfect
In every word
Be perfect
In every action"

It was the weight of a planet
Thick black and dark
Upon my heart.

I cried out
From the core of a world
Knowing only a god could hear me.
And hear me he did.

His eyes pierced the blackness
And ears heard me from prison.

From lips a universe away
Came a piercing whisper

"You are my son,
You are enough."

His arm stretched from heaven
And his finger touched me
In my very heart.

Light erupted from the core of the world
And ripped through the blackness.
Every "you have to be"
Every "you should have"
Every "you absolutely must"
Buckled under the voice of God
And was replaced.

I am enough
I am ENOUGH
I AM ENOUGH

Cry it from the rooftops
Sing it in every land!
Though it once was black and lifeless,
The world now shines bright with glory.
Tell it to every demon and fiend
On the face of this earth,
Let the angels come again
And make this place God's footstool.

I am enough.
I am not perfect, ideal or flawless
And I cannot hope to be so

In this life.

I am, nevertheless
ENOUGH,
Because I am a son of God
Unconditionally deserving
Of His mighty love.

And I will stand Before God,
My Father

And He and I will agree
I am enough.

I have peace today
And can have peace again,
Crying ceaselessly to my God
Striving endlessly to grow,
Not from the stress of shame
Nor the threat of hell,
But because of a love of myself
And a desire to grow like my God
I will press forward in faith,.
Remembering each day
The promise: I am enough.

Facing Demons

I cannot write
I think
About slaying demons.
For mine are alive and well.

But I can write of facing demons
And staring down
That which I hate most about myself,
Wondering how it might be killed
Without destroying the whole.

I perceive too
That destroying a demon,
Removing it from power in my body
Might of necessity diminish me

For my greatest strengths
Share their roots
With my strongest evils.

Perhaps my ordeal
Of killing demons is wrong then
But I must face my demons
And find in them the heart that beats

In time with mine.

Perhaps instead of facing demons
I must face God,
Who knows my heart and mind
Better than I.
It is He who said
"If my people come unto me
I will make their weaknesses strengths"
It is He who will make
Of the hosts of fiends in me
A royal army.

I trust the change
Will not come in a day
And yet I trust
That that which is bitter in my life
Will one day be just the right spice.
That which I most desire to hide
Will fill me with righteous pride.
That which drags me to the abyss
Will be the very tool by which I lift
And bless and help
Those around me.

I cannot kill my demons
And will no more face them
But I will face my God
Who can sanctify my soul

And change the face of my demons
From stygian black
To glittering gold.

I Knelt

I knelt before my bed
No,
My God,
Who felt so distant
That dark night.
About me was my sin;
A black snake
Constricting my soul.
But a dim flame of faith
Through the shame caught hold
So I raised my voice and prayed
To the God who is mighty to save.

He sent a change
The air became dank
And the ground hard.

I knelt before a crib,
No,
A manger.
In it was a baby,
With brilliant blue eyes.
Before me was the Christ.
I cried.
In the infant's eyes, I saw

Nascent mercy
And wisdom abounding.
His eyes seemed to search me
And say,
"I know you
Personally."

The serpent hissed
Yet I could see
Light beginning to pour
Back into me.

I prayed more,
In the name of the Babe
To Our Father above.

Again came a change,
Rain fell upon my back.
Mud squished beneath my knees.

I knelt before a tree.
No, a cross.
On it hung a man
With sad blue eyes.
Before me was the Christ.
Again, I cried.
In the Savior's eyes, I saw
Profound pain
And relentless love.

He looked to heaven and said,
"Father, forgive him,
Although he knows
What he has done."

The snake climbed
To fight the Christ
But as it touched his holy blood,
Which flowed from his pale, pierced feet,
Black scales fell away,
And slowly, painfully,
The snake became gold.
My guilt and shame
Were swept away.
I saw a smile
On my Savior's face.

With glittering gold
The snake came,
And embraced me.
Though I didn't move,
At that moment I left hell.
Both the prison of shame
That held me bound for years,
And that painful hill
Whereon my Savior was killed.
I was in a new place when I looked up,
Gold and bright,
Peaceful.

I knelt before a man.
No, a God
Who stood on scarred feet,
And looked at me
With loving eyes.
Before me was the Christ.
I wept and washed his feet
With tears.
In my Savior's eyes, I saw,
Profound peace,
and incomprehensible glory.
He looked at me and said,
"Welcome home, my son,
Enter into my rest."

I blinked and again knelt
Before my bed,
My God
And the snake,
Who had become gold, guiltless and pure.
My heart filled with all manner
Of love and emotion,
And into it came a voice:
"That is your end, my son.
Please, for me, endure,
For you have a light
To carry to a darkened world.
You carry the truth of my love

The promise of hope
The power of faith.
No longer droop in sin,
Rejoice in the gospel
And share the good news:
I am risen from death,
And you will arise.
No one need stay
In the black of night.
Available to all
Is my healing light."

So now I say to you,
In the name of the Babe,
The Crucified,
The Christ,
Come and be saved,
Come and receive eternal life.

To Lucifer

How art thou fallen from heaven!
O Lucifer, thou son of the morning!
How art thou cut low to the ground,
Which did weaken the nations!
You were our brother there,
Before the foundation of the earth
In God's heavenly courts!
You were our friend,
And we grew with you!
And yet you seek to make us all miserable,
Like unto yourself.

O Lucifer, what glory
Could have been yours,
If only you had not set your heart
On a throne above that of our Dear Father.

What lies you spread, O Lucifer,
To divide they who once were your
Friends, sisters, and brothers
Both from each other,
And from the Living God,
The Merciful Father of us all.

You say the sword of justice

Gleams over the righteous.
You make the arms of mercy
Seem closed to they who are oh so deserving
Of their Savior's sweet embrace.
You make us feel that the Lord lies when he says
"The worth of souls is great
In the sight of God,"
You cause us to forget
That every knee will bow
And every tongue confess
That his works in eternity
Are perfect,
Just, merciful, loving,
And never amiss.

O Lucifer thou crafty liar
O Lucifer thou father of lies
I pity thee and thy benighted estate.
Yet I defy thee, in the name of Jesus.
And I will fight thee endlessly
By the blood of the Lamb,
Which is relentless mercy,
And by the word of my testimony,
Which is faith, hope, and charity.
I will not be cast down,
I will not be bound to lies,
I will stand exalted
On the great and last day,
And thou, Lucifer,

Will cry out from thy eternal abode
With weeping, wailing
And gnashing of teeth.

All the days of my life,
I will speak in the name of the Almighty
Among my brothers and sisters,
Who once were yours, O Lucifer,
And the word of the Lord my God
Will pierce thy lies
As a sword through the web
Of a forsaken spider.

We may fall,
We may faint,
We may fail.
But we are of the house of Israel,
We are the sons of Abraham,
Isaac and Jacob.
We are the children of Christ.
And know thou, our fallen brother,
The God of Israel will prevail.

To the Enslaved People of the Oak Valley Plantation

Chattel
Substance
Property.

Verily,
O children of God
You were more,
You are more,
To me,
And to our Lord.

Your soul is more,
For the Son of our God
Gave his perfect self
For your salvation.

Your bonds in life sadden me,
And stain this nation
Which claims to be founded on freedom
But was deeply founded on your blood, sweat,
and tears

But hear my brother

And sing my sister
The hands of Jesus
Have broken any cords
That could hold you bound.
Christ will set us free from sin
And give liberation from death.

You who once were slaves
May be kings and priests
Queens and priestesses
Unto the most high God,
Clothed no more in rags,
But in the robes of royalty
No longer to suffer under slavery
For we will live together in unity
With the God whose name is Love.

He will wipe away all tears
And repay tenfold the suffering of this life
With an eternal weight of glory.

A Reminder

You are not alone.
You may be struggling,
You may be lonely,
You may be despairing,
But I must remind you,
You are not alone.
From the scriptures I've come to know
That Jesus Christ fell below
Every conceivable blow.
He's been stabbed and scourged and spat upon.
During his life he wept and mourned and cried.
But Christ did not give in.
To win the fight, he gave up his life
And took it up again.

And because of him,
My dearest friend,
You are not alone.

Jesus Christ
Is alive.
Nails pierced through his hands and feet;
A sword stabbed in his side,
Upon the Roman's cross he died

Yet from the tomb he did rise
And now he stands alive.

By the power of our Father
He burst death's cords asunder.
By His infinite suffering
He extended an arm of endless mercy.
Christ's dark tomb is empty
His throne is filled with light.
If we listen we will hear him
His voice ever calls us in the night.
"Come unto me" He cries,
"Come and live in the bright sunlight,
Amidst endless streams of mercy.
Receive the gift for which I died,
Come and receive eternal life"

Perfectionism

You don't have to be perfect
You just have to give
What you have,
Whether what you have
Is a semi full of food
Or a few flakey loaves.
In the hand of the Lord,
Anything is enough.

This is not just a principle
For feeding five thousand;
Truly this teaching
Applies to everything.
No person is perfect, complete or whole on their
own.
But they who follow the Son of God
Have a perfect leader as their guide,
And a perfect helper at their side.

If we want to go where he is,
To live with him where he lives
We need to walk the way
That he first trod.

Nevertheless, remember, my friend,

You don't have to walk perfectly
When you walk with the son of God.

You just have to learn humility,
To stop when he says "stop"
To move when he says "move"
To change when he says "change"
And take his hand when he offers it.

It also takes the patience
To remember that you'll fail.
You'll go when he says stop
You'll run when he says walk
You'll stumble and fall a lot.
That doesn't mean you're worthless
That doesn't mean you're useless
That just means you're normal.

No matter how many times you fail
No matter how many times you fall
No matter how far you find yourself
From the beaten trail
Take the hand of the Savior
Let him brush you off
Let him wipe your tears
Let him take you back
And walk with you a while,
With this soft reminder:
"You'll make it home one day."

Don't obsess over every flaw
Don't fixate on every wrong
You may miss everything
That your Savior bought.
His fingers traced the valleys
His whisper raised the mountains
His love sent the rain and sun.
Each and every part
Of this great life of yours
Is for your growth
And for your good.
No strong tree grew in a day.
No mighty lion hunts alone.
No gold is purified without fire.
The Lord will make you
More strong,
More mighty
and more pure
Than all of these.
We don't know what he's given
So we can fail
We don't know what he's given
For us to mess up.
We don't know what he's given
To help us succeed.
But we know that he's given
His nail-scarred hands
For us to take hold

And never look back.
Take his hand, my friend,
Walk the walk with him
Fail and succeed fearlessly,
To one day live with him
Endlessly.

Open My Bones

Open my bones and weep
For in this sepulcher
You will not find that which you seek.

All my money is gone,
That which you thought was yours
For I searched your soul for good
And found none.

Open my bones and weep
And as your tears stream
Like a river down your face

Let them remind you
Of the choice, you have to make,
For you can join me here in death
Known forever as the son of a great one
A new king Tut
Taken too soon.

But I know you have it in you
My dearest son,
Who weeps not for his father's bones
But for the loss of his own inheritance:
You can be great on your own.

Purity is not in your heart
But potential is in your mind,
Truth which leads to eternal life.

This loss is a gift
If you take of these bones,
Your tears and the fire of your soul
And rise from this tomb
Determined to become
A better man than I ever was.

It is your choice, my boy.
Open my bones,
And weep.

The Body of a God

Lay on a table
At the head of the chapel.
His flesh lay torn on trays
His blood poured into cups
So that we each might have a piece.

One might think
These faithful saints
Would be struck with grief
Eating the body of their God
But it was clear to see
That on each face was peace.

The flesh was but bread,
For God had said
"I am the bread
Of life"
And the blood was water
For he told his people
"I am the living waters"

And though His body lay
On the table of the sacrament
God Himself yet reigns,
With an enthroned, immortal body

And through this symbol feast
We remember both
The blood and body he gave
On our behalf
And the eternal life we can have.
Life like his, with him
For in eating him, we put on Christ.
He becomes us
And we become him.
He takes our weakness and sin,
When we lay them on him,
And He gives us his goodness and perfection
When we receive the sacrament.

David and Goliath

The man stood tall,
Rippling with muscle,
Breathing heavily, his body filled
With a lust for blood.

It pleased Goliath to see
The mass of men flee
At his own mighty presence.

He had watched for forty days,
The armies of Israel scrambling
For someone willing to fight a giant.

He had seen a few large men
Among the Hebrews.
Each one excited him,
He would love to crush the skull
Of the mightiest man they had.

Today they finally sturred
And sent one forth
To face the mountain of a man.

Instead of their great men, they sent a small one,
A boy, really

Who looked to be a shepherd.

Goliath didn't see it,
But the boy David
Had a fire in his eyes.

"You think me a sheep,
And come to me with a crook?"
Goliath cried, incredulous.

"You think me a dog,
And come to me with a stick?"
Bellowed the giant,
The goliath Goliath.

"Come here, young boy
And I will feed your flesh
To the fowls of the air!"

The boy's face showed pure determination
He looked to the man,
Who imbued fear in his nation

"You come to me with a sword and spear,
You threaten me with a javelin,"
Spake David, the farm boy,
Himself armed with stones.
"But I come to you in the name
Of the King of Heaven,

The Lord of Hosts,
The God of the armies of Israel"

David cried, unshaken,
"You have defied these chosen armies,
The name of Jehovah himself!
So God will deliver you into my hands
And I will take your head this day
As a witness to the whole earth
That there is a living God
And He is with my people, Israel."

Goliath cursed David
In the name of the Philistine deities
And charged the boy
With more indignation than perhaps
He ever felt in his life.

David didn't fear this man
For his heart was filled
With the power of God.
Where any man would turn and flee
David ran towards the one
Who could end his life so easily.

From David's cloth emerged
A single fist-sized rock.
He swung his sling with all his might
And gave that rock a shot.

It found its target, clean and true
The forehead of a monster, it flew to.

With a smack and a crash
A miracle was wrought,
That Goliath, who could slay any man
To the ground dropped
Because of a shepherd's rock.

The Apostle to the Apostles

Mary was at once like all of us
And yet in a position no one else could garner
There, when she saw the gardener.

For all of us,
At some point,
Walk through the valley of the shadow of death,
Fearing evil, feeling grief,
Or flaming with rage.

And she, likely, felt them all at once
At the loss of a man she loved,
Who had taught her tenderly
And blessed her deeply.
In his stead she knew
Barrabus, a murderer,
Yet breathed and walked free.
While her master and teacher
Hung from a tree on Calvary,
And laid in a tomb.

We all have felt these in some measure
And yet at some point,
Our capacity to empathize cannot descend to
meet her.

For the perfect man,
In whom there was no sin or guile,
This man who did only good
And who showed her a heaven
Far more beautiful than she had even imagined,
That Perfect Man,
Doubtless the Very Son of God,
Was betrayed by his closest friend
And tried by cruel and corrupted courts,
And sentenced to die by a mass of people
Who she knew he loved
With every single fiber of his being.

And this was how her heart broke
When she thought to herself
"After all this, Lord,
They will take away from me
Even his dead body?"

How much more relieved must she have been,
When the gardener knew her name
And she knew his voice,
One smooth as a river
And warm as a bonfire.

How quickly the world changed
In that moment when she could say with
certainty

"Rabboni, you're alive!"
It was a sunrise after weeks of night.

Sweet Mary Magdalene
Was the first of all mortals
To see one of their own made immortal.
She is the first great Apostle,
The first witness to the resurrection.
Surely she stands today
Clothed with power from the Highest
To continue to bear witness,
"Jesus Christ came to earth
Took upon him all sin,
Died upon the cross at Calvary
And rose from the grave,
First coming to me."

A Boy Seeking Truth

He was a boy surrounded
By a furious war of words.
Palmyra ablaze in the fervent heat
Of the Great Awakening;
Preacher, teacher, and convert
Each fighting to prove their church
The truest of them all.

Joseph Smith then sought truth,
For he thirsted after it.
He sought the church with whom
He could feel and shout like the rest
And more deeply, the church
Where he could go
To find remission of sins
And salvation for his soul.

"Lo, here is Christ!"
They cried
"Lo, there is Christ!"
They shouted.
"Lo, where is Christ?"
Asked Joseph.
It was impossible, said he,
For a boy of fourteen

To find the truth of anything,
Until he found a verse piercing
James 1:5, a veritable light
Saying, "if any of you lack wisdom,
Let him ask of God
Who giveth to all men liberally
And upbraideth not"

It struck Joseph that the truth
Was held not by a pastor or a preacher.
No, the true church
Could not be found by asking any man,
No matter how many times he's read the Bible.
To receive the truth,
Pure, unadulterated,
It must come from the pure,
Perfect lips of the living God.

So in the woods, he sought Him
Who is the source of all truth
And the light of the world.

Joseph found a place alone,
Beneath the watch of the mighty trees,
The bright sun, and the fresh flowers.
He knelt on the forest floor,
And spoke aloud in prayer to God,
Saying that prayer which millions
Before and since have said:

"To whom shall I go
To save my soul?"

His voice roused the forces
Of both heaven and hell,
And hell came first.
The forest darkened
And the boy's tongue thickened
A being from the deep,
Of power astonishing
Tried to force his prayer to cease.
His mind filled with evil thoughts
And he heard the sound
Of an invisible someone
Running through the dried leaves.
His heart sank within him,
Despair filled his chest,
But he called upon God
With all energy of heart
Nearly but never losing faith.
At the very moment he thought he was gone
He looked up to see a light,
A fire descending from the sky.
A pillar that turned the green leaves
To a brilliant gold as it descended upon his head.
Hell and darkness fled,
And when the light touched him,
His being filled with peace and joy.
The glory of the Lord was upon him,

As it was with Moses, and the prophets.
Soon, within that light
Appeared the most glorious figures
Joseph Smith had ever seen.
Not one God but two;
In form like men,
With robes whiter than snow
And faces brighter than the sun.
With a voice like a rushing river
One addressed him
And pointed to his companion,

"Joseph, this is my beloved Son,
Hear Him."

Before Joseph's eyes
Were his Heavenly Father
And his Savior, Jesus Christ
Who's scars were still visible
In his hands, feet, and side.

A deeper wave of peace
Swept over the boy as the Savior
Personally forgave him of his sins.

Then they permitted him to speak
"Which of all the churches is true?
Which of them do you approve?"

The Lord forbid him to join any
"They draw near to me with their lips,
But their hearts are far from me,
They teach for doctrines
The commandments of men,
Having a form of godliness,
But they deny the power thereof."

The Lord revealed many things
To the boy Joseph there.
Many angels came to speak
And minister to him.
He kept those secrets tight.

The vision closed, he was left alone
A mind full of wonder,
A heart full of love.
He knew in truth
That none of all the churches
Were ones he could go to.
And yet he knew
That the creator of the world
Knew his name and heard his prayer.

So much followed this boy-turned-prophet of
God.
Hell ceased not to fight against him
And great became the army
Who opposed those who bore witness

That the Lord spoke to men today.
But great too became the church
Founded by a prophet
Who spoke with God like Moses
Face to face.
It stands still today
The Church of Jesus Christ
Of Latter-day Saints.

Hear my voice,
Oh, ends of the earth,
Jesus Christ is the Son of God,
Who lives and speaks today.
Joseph Smith Jr. saw him
And talked with him on many occasions.
God ceased not to call prophets,
And in an unbroken line
The authority and call
Have fallen today to another,
Russell M Nelson.

Through these men
God speaks to the whole world
And by their guidance
We can connect with God
Every saint for themselves.

Seek for yourself the answer
Which Joseph Smith himself sought

"Which of all the churches is true?"
Today there is one,
Which stands on the foundation
Which Christ himself laid
Of prophets and apostles.

The Nature of Mankind

The scriptures say that Jesus
Is coeternal with the Father,
Endless and eternal in both directions.

And lo the Lord revealed this truth
To Joseph Smith
And a few key prophets
That like a ring around a finger,
To give one a beginning is to make and end,
And so a wholly created man,
One with a finite beginning,
Will eventually have an end.

"God Himself,"
Joseph said
"Could not create himself."

Nor could he,
From nothing,
Create you,
For in doing so,
And making a true beginning,
He would create your end.

These are deep waters,
Understood only dimly,
But they give the key to eternity.

God calls the origin of you and me
In our mortal, broken language,
Intelligence.
A substance that cannot be created,
But was from the beginning,
And will never end.
That is the seed, the core
From which God shaped mankind.

I repeat,
If Joseph Smith is right,
And did speak with God face to face,
There is something in you
That has always been you
In all of endless time.
And our Heavenly Father
Clothed you in spirit
And your parents here
Clothed you in flesh.

And if God made a world
Where creatures bring forth after their kind
And God has called us His children
Then we are after his kind.

In the words of the prophet Lorenzo Snow
"As God now is, man may become,
As man now is, God once was."

Like a caterpillar cannot see in itself
The butterfly that lies within,
We cannot see within ourselves
The eternal glory under our skins.

But it is there,
Though not observable with microscopes,
Or any instrument of mortal science,
It is there,
And one who is humble
And faithful
And seeks to know God
Will find they feel His Spirit
Communing with their own

And He will confirm
To the willing heart and seeking mind
At the right time
That they have, in their celestial DNA,
The potential to become like God,
To love with boundless depth
To bless others with infinite light
To create unfathomable beauty for all within
reach.
And you may think,

If a man received the power of God
Would he not do evil with it?

And in that question of abuse of power
We find the path to true, eternal power.
Here is a key to becoming like God.

Any who has power tantamount to God's
Must have evil purged from their soul
Every single iota.
It is only in a vessel filled with pure love
That God can pour in his fulness.
For God is love
And they who love so purely
That it becomes their unchanging identity
Become like God,
To spend the rest of eternity
Filled with infinite power, wisdom, and might,
And to spend the rest of time
Filling others with that same light.

Tear-stained plates

Surely those golden plates
On which was written the first draft
Of the Book of Mormon,
Were bathed in the tears of great men,
Who saw tragedy among their people.

Did Joseph Smith see those tearstains
As he translated the plates?

Did Joseph see the tears
Of Nephi and Moroni?
Of that little brother, made prophet,
Who watched, in vision, his seed
War and prosper;
Who watched his offspring
Hear and hold the resurrected Savior.
Nephi saw centuries fly by
And watched great men rise up,
To serve God in unity and love
To create a society without poor.
But oh the tears he must have shed
As he watched their children,
Who took upon themselves
The names of Nephi and of Christ,
Enter into deals with the devil

And create secret combinations with Satan.
He watched them turn from hunger and thirst for
righteousness
To a lust for blood.
He watched the fruits of their repentence
Turn ripe with iniquity.
He watched them turn from the height of faith
To irredeemable doubt,
Such that the the Lord
Could withhold justice no longer.
So this faithful servant of God watched
His flesh and blood a millenium away
Annihilate themselves with war and hate.

Surely Joseph saw and felt
The sadness of this first Nephite,
Nephi himself,
As he translated the plates.
Surely, too he felt the grief and pain
Of that last Nephite, Moroni
Who was there personally
To witness the Nephite annihilation.
Moroni fought in the fight that would turn
Their final thousands and ten thousands
To twenty five remaining Nephites.
He heard the voice of his father
Crying out to the souls
Of those poor men, women and children who
could have known the Lord

And found salvation in his arms.
These people, who's fathers had seen the face of
Jesus Christ,
And felt the scars in his hands;
Who's fathers saw angels from heaven
And heard them speak in a language
Known only by them who live in the presence of
the living God.
Yet the children of the faithful
Would not come unto the Master.
They trampled him under their feet,
They walked by their own sparks,
And they sought vengeance over their brethren
Until the battlefield was full of blood and gore,
And their enemies stood firm
Only to hunt down those last twenty five
Who took the name of Nephi.
And so cried out Mormon,
The faithful father of Moroni:
"O ye fair ones,
How could ye have departed
From the ways of the Lord!
O ye fair ones,
How could ye have rejected that Jesus,
Who stood with open arms to receive you!
Behold, if ye had not done this,
Ye would not have fallen.
But behold, ye are fallen,
And I mourn your loss.

O ye fair sons and daughters,
Ye fathers and mothers,
Ye husbands and wives,

Ye fair ones!

How is it that ye could have fallen!
O that ye had repented before
This great destruction had come upon you."

Mormon too would shortly be killed,
Leaving his son Moroni,
The final man of faith
On the entire continent.
The Lamanites were vicious, merciless,
And because of their hatred
They put to death every Nephite
That would not deny the Christ.
Yet with boldness, with power,
And with great faith he wrote
"I, Moroni, will not deny the Christ;"
So he wandered, and wondered
When the Father would call him home.
When he could end his mortal journey,
Be set free of his isolation
And live with the just in paradise.
Never did he give up,
Never did his faith fail,
Never did he cease to endure.

He finished his writing to the world
With this testimony:

"God shall show unto you,
That that which I have written is true.
Please, come unto Christ,
And lay hold upon every good gift,
Come unto Christ,
And be perfected in him,
Deny yourselves of all ungodliness;
Love God with all your might, mind and
strength,
Then is his grace sufficient for you,
That ye may be perfect in Christ.
I bid unto all, farewell.
I soon go to rest in the paradise of God,
Until my spirit and body shall reunite,
Brought forth triumphant through the air,
To meet you before the pleasing bar
Of the great Jehovah, the Eternal Judge"

Surely they met one day,
In the courts of heaven,
Nephi, Moroni and Joseph,
Together, immortal, glorified,
Together they mourned and rejoiced
Over the broad history of the Nephites,
And all the children of Father.
Their work is not yet done

But those great men
Will never again suffer as they did
In their mortal life.
Yet they will still cry
Over the lives of you and I
With joy as we succeed
And despair at our defeat.
So press forward, my friend
The power of faith
And the strength of our friends
Will carry us onward
To join them in heaven.

What Remains

I was on my knees that night,
My family's home lay in shambles,
Smoke yet rising to the thundering sky,
Like incense to an angry god.

"When the hard times come,
When tragedy strikes you,
And it will" dad had said,
"Always be grateful for what remains."

His voice rang in my head,
Hurting me with every echo.
I knew in my heart already,
I was all that remained of my family.

I didn't have time-
Not in the blinding flash,
The deafening crash,
The sudden, searing blaze-
To grab things or people.
I could only run, our house went up so fast;
Burning wood falling behind me,
Leaving all I loved trapped.

I looked to the sky and wept and cried.

Storm clouds drizzled rain
And crackled with malicious thunder.
Pitiful rain and mighty wind
All conspired to stoke the flames.
That was all God gave me
The night he took away everything.

Then came a stream of lights and faces and
questions.
Firemen put out the fire,
Trying to save my family,
Though all they could do
Was carry out the corpses.

Policemen assessed the situation,
My body explaining the lightning to them
While my mind resigned to the back.
If I could have left that shattered reality,
And joined the corpses of my family
I would have in a heartbeat.

Paramedics took my vitals
But my body wasn't hurt
There was nothing they could do for me
Unless they could raise the dead.

My aunt and uncle came to my rescue
And took me away for a few days.
They were my first angels,

Taking on the things a kid should not.

I was mature then,
Or so I thought.
That very day I had wondered
If life would be easier for me
All on my own.
The answer the lightning gave
Was no.

My aunt and uncle,
They dealt with the estate
And the grim funeral.

Yet they could not take away my pain,
They couldn't ease my bitter grief.
They prayed with me, and for me
But I couldn't pray with them.
I couldn't pray to a God
Who would take everything from me in an
instant.

***

Eventually, they took me back
To see if we could find anything
In what remained.

They let me go in first, alone.

The sight of the rubble again,
The memory of that night,
The crash of thunder and the screams
All fell back on top of me.

I collapsed and cried,
Dissolving into that dark, stormy night.
But then I felt someone at my side.
I looked to see my dad, dressed in white.

"We still remain,"
He said,
"We love you so much,
Your mother, your brothers and I.
I cannot stay long, my daughter.
But know that we still remain,
And we will wait for you here.
We will be with you and
You will be great."

I stood up to go to him,
I wanted nothing more
Than to feel his arms around me,
But I took my eyes off him for a moment
And he was gone.

"Dad?" I called,
"Dad? Where did you go?"

"I'm still here,"
Came his voice,
Not to my ears but my heart.
The impenetrable darkness,
The freezing cold night
That had shaken my soul to the core,
Was replaced by a rising sun.
A warm morning. Hope.

New tears came now,
Not agonizing sobs
But soft tears.
I felt, for the first time,
Pure peace.

I found in my house preserved, somehow
Many pictures of my family.
I knew that they were near.
And though my life would yet have bitter days
And difficult years,
I never stopped to testify
That my family was still here.
I will return to them one day.
Until then I will live,
Grateful that they still remain.

Near the Veil

There was a man I met
Near the veil
His mind drifted like a butterfly
Swept in a shifting wind,
From past,
To present,
To, it seemed,
The future.
For at times, the wind swept him up
Beyond the veil that separates the physical
From the spiritual world.
He spoke then
In those fleeting moments
With the dead who were gathered there
To greet him when he went.

Other times the wind would ease
And he would come out
And speak with perfect clarity
And say to me "Isn't she pretty?"
But then dementia heaved again.
And the butterfly was put to flight.

He spent nights
In the past, on the wing

On his feet, teaching a class.
His students had all grown
His position had been filled
He had long since retired.
Yet he stood at night
Teaching the air
How to read a ruler.
You could hear his love for the kids
You could see in his eyes
He wanted the best for them.
But then it was midnight
And his wife needed sleep.
She got it, eventually.

I feel in the world hopelessness.
What does it matter if this man was good?
What does it matter if this man gave his heart to
those around him?
What does it matter if he never thought of
himself?
What does his good heart matter,
If all that was waiting for him
Was dark, dementia ridden nights?
The world asks these questions
To a godless sky
The world asks these questions
To an unforgiving universe.
The world asks these questions
To equations, axioms, and theorums.

But I know the source to go to for answers
Of an eternal nature.
He is our Eternal Father, even God.
He is the God who made the sky,
The God who shaped the universe
The God who sent his Son
To die for all mankind, that they might save
All the works of their hands.
God lives. I know it in my soul.
And though my friend has died,
And though I will die,
And though the earth will die
Like sawdust in a fire,
I know by revelation from God,
That death is not the end.
For the Son of God died,
And rose again.

Verily, death is not the end.
For Jesus Christ will come again
Bearing the light of resurrection.
My friend and I will rise,
Along with everyone we ever loved.
And Lo, we will be unchained,
From every mortal pain.

We will grow in wisdom and stature,
And if faithful, we will lay hold

On life eternal.
The very kind of life God lives.
This is the end of life,
Not a conclusive end
But a purposeful end.

And now my friend,
I invite you,
To come unto Him,
Even Jesus.
Learn of Him
Walk in his paths.
You will have peace in this life
And a glorious resurrection
In the sweet by and by.
There is no sin so dark,
That the Savior can't make it white.
There is no burden too heavy
That the Savior can't make it light.
Look to him and live,
For He lives; he is the Christ.

Tearing Axioms

The day had been written of for ages
And I had read many of the texts.

For weeks I had considered the signs,
So many things had lined up
With the words of prophets and the sects.
But I held it as an axiom
That these were just
The traditions of dead ages.

And yet I lived somehow to see
All those things fulfilled.

The wicked burned as stubble,
The righteous raised from the grave,
Mountains bowing to One
Who came with sword in hand
To tear down the axioms of men

He came to raise up the valleys of dead,
And exalt the poor in spirit,
And magnify the mighty in faith.

I cannot describe the feelings in my heart,
The loss of colleagues

Whom I loved despite their many flaws,
The gain of loved ones,
My dear grandparents,
My sweet wife
And dear daughter
All of whom I thought
Surely were gone forever.

For better or for worse
Jesus Christ tore down the axioms
Which I had held unquestioned.

***

Today I saw His face
Now I know He knows my name

He taught me tenderly
Of His mighty grace
And His love for those who passed away

This mighty man,
This Deity
Even He spurns at the thought
Of one suffering for eternity.

He asked me to join his cause
And lift my voice with his,
Seeking out the lost,

To teach them to yield their axioms
And put their trust in God.

He told me then, that
They who repent
And change with their might and mind
Will find in turn redeeming light.
All they who worked wickedly on earth
Could learn the Lord's law in the spirit
And rise again to dwell with the just
Gratefully spared from eternal hell.

On worthlessness

Know this,
You who feel worthless
You are bought with a price.
Even the life of Jesus Christ.
You may not feel of any worth
But for you
He bore the whole earth.

I have, at times, felt like trash,
Valued as a pile of ash,
Barely worth a second glance.
And in those times
When my only desire,
Is to drift away,
As smoke in a fire,
I seek peace on my knees.

You should know, dear friend,
Heaven has heard me,
And came to my aid.
My sweet Savior ran
And wrapped me his soft embrace.

His Holy Spirit whispered,
"The God of the universe

Bled and died for you.
It was his plan for you to fail,
For you to fall
for you to feel
Pain, fear and suffering.
God knew the only way
You could rise to heights sublime,
Is first to dive into the night.
Then His great sacrifice
Would create redeeming light,
And as you ask for his might,
He would lift you to eternal heights."
Christ whispers now to me,
That to you I should repeat this gospel sweet.
And so I say in simplicity,
The God of Heaven loves you, truly.

www.ingramcontent.com/pod-product-compliance
Lightning Source LLC
Chambersburg PA
CBHW070550160726
48003CB00005B/1971